Under The Cedar Tree

poetry for every season

Leah Marie Waller

Cover Illustration by Arwin Lieb

1st WORLD
PUBLISHING

Under The Cedar Tree

Leah Marie Waller

Cover Illustration by Arwin Lieb

© Leah Marie Waller 2008

Published by 1stWorld Publishing
P.O. Box 2211, Fairfield, IA 52556
tel: 641-209-5000 • fax: 866-440 5234
web: www.1stworldpublishing.com

First Edition

LCCN: 2008929094
SoftCover ISBN: 978-1-4218-9887-2
HardCover ISBN: 978-1-4218-9886-5
eBook ISBN: 978-1-4218-9888-9

Dedicated to my Grandfather,
Guy Everett Johnson Jr.,
for his love, kindness, inspiration
and poetic genius…

Special Thanks To...

My mother, Springli Johnson,
an example of endless love, compassion and elegance.
My father, Michael Pinkel,
a true serving of inspiration, creativity and happiness.
My stepfather, Robert Johnson,
a man of unpredictable and irreplaceable wisdom.
My sisters and brothers, Arwin, Sam, Mira, Ben,
Nicky, Sammy and Essa, for being a reliable source
of support and laughter.
Josh, for always helping, holding and believing in me
from cover to cover
Melanny, Cat and all my beloved friends,
for putting up with a hopeless romantic.
My wonderful and unforgettable grandparents.
My dedicated and charming co-workers,
I'd never be here without your nagging.
The masters of poetry and the big shoes
they left on my doorstep.
Nynke Passi and all of the teachers
who guided my pen and stretched my talents.
To you, the reader, for supporting the timeless, simple
beauty of poetry.
And to you my fellow poet; never forget you have a gift
and never stop using it.

Table of Contents

SUMMER

FALL

WINTER

Introduction

This drunkenness began in some tavern.
When I get back around to that place, I'll be completely sober.

—Rumi

It starts over a blank page. My pen is drawn like an inky weapon; my mind is peaceful—then, suddenly, in the opaque rectangular oblivion, appears all of creation. I struggle for a moment, panicking at the sea of potential and then my mind begins to focus. It condenses to experiences and then thoughts, it flies past sentences and, just as it is hovering around words, I manage to take hold and scratch out some organized letters. The rest of the poem flows out from that first word. Each thought balances on the previous like an artistic puzzle.

I have written this book for many reasons, but the first and foremost is to honor the beautiful, tragically fading, tradition of poetry. Somehow, many years ago, when the world decided to "get real," some jaded group of confused misfits agreed that the "real" life was about money and power instead of smiles and romance. I have been called a "hopeless romantic" so many times in my life I could sew a dress from those words, but I am more than willing to continue on in my ways for the good of the heart of the human race. I believe that poetry serves an inexplicable purpose in our lives and it should never, at any cost, die out.

The craft and comprehension of the poetic language will always be one of my favorite things in the world. Somehow in the curves and lines of words I have found my way to heaven and there is no reason to relocate.

Spring...

"A book is only a hearts portrait, every page a pulse."

—Emily Dickenson

Under The Cedar Tree

Held by the spring shadows of this silent cedar tree,
the open world above me takes long blue cloudless breaths
and curious cicadas hum around my overturned sleeping bag.
The thick roots
and hushing dust
are more the sky
than the ground.
I can't find the bird
in the branches,
but I can taste
the lilacs
in the breeze.
A car beeps,
a child laughs.
It's good to be
barefoot again.

Where Is My Poem

Where is my poem?
I must have been too needy for him.
I demanded that we spend every evening together,
so one day he said that he was going out
for a pack of smokes
and never came back.

I saw him in a dance club months later
flirting with other poets
and he looked so good—
lines cut in a sharp buzz,
his images even more direct and clear.
A cigar stuck in his mouth
like a fork in a pie
as he cleanly told me
he was done.

I stood on the other side of the glass
watching him dance with the other poets.
He saw me and, feeling guilty,
put on his black fedora
and came out into the street light.
He said, "What do you want?
Can't you see I'm busy?"
I said, "I came for my passion,
hand it over, and we'll be done here."

Leah Marie Waller

He placed it in my hands
wrapped in a small couplet.
But no sooner had he touched me
than he wanted more.
He held me in iambic pentameter,
tangled my hair into simile and metaphor.
He kissed me uncontrollably.
Wet lips pulsing stanza after stanza,
he filled my page.
Then he pulled away,
went back inside to dance with the other poets.
leaving me
with only
a page of words.

When the Rain Stops

When the rain stops, all the oak cottages and brick houses
open their windows and the tulips pucker at the sky.

When the rain stops, petals, twigs and leaves race each other
down the sides of the clean streets.

The neighborhood children mingle over four square
  and watermelon,
while the grey puddle water rolls around and bows off their
  tiny yellow boots.

When the rain stops, the tired evening sun
rests her fuzzy peach head
on the dripping roof tops
and tosses her wild hair
into the clouds.

Balconies reach, living rooms shrink,
the trees click their brittle nails at the wind.
Sunroofs open like curtains to stages of operatic birds.
A tall skinny woman takes down a bun of thick almond hair.
Just as soon as the rain stops falling
  on this little Midwestern town.

Leah Marie Waller

A Room for Poetry

A tiny room with castle panes tucked in an Irish wood
if you don't already have one I'm telling you, you should.

A tattered cup with eighty pens, each pulping endless ink
and stain glass windows streaming purple
  tossed in shades of pink.

A cedar cupboard in the back that's filled with unctuous snacks
and little fairies gliding through with magic at their backs.

Ivy walls and fuzzy balls and secret book knob doors
granddad clocks with cooing birds and lushy carpet floors

The smell of laundry freshly tumbled lined in limber rose
and naked paintings stroked in tan each in a crooked pose.

Childhood

Those black rain boots
With the yellow stripe and the hole
That red sweater with the ripping cuffs
And candy I was never suppose to have
Skinned knees to heal and skin again
Toy boats to ride through bathtub seas
Graveyard sandboxes to bury toys alive
And candy I always ate anyways
Big sisters to tell on
The whole world in the back yard
Dogs to convince my parents to buy
And candy that always made me sick

Leah Marie Waller

What Is Great Poetry?

The most beautiful and most profound emotion we can experience is the sensation of the mystical. It is the sower of all true art and science. He to whom this emotion is a stranger, who can no longer wonder and stand rapt in awe, is as good as dead.

—Albert Einstein

When a friend asked me what the definition of great poetry was, my deep love and appreciation for the poetic world worked against me. I had an extremely difficult time narrowing down what I considered the best of a great subject. It was as if someone had asked me, "What is an apple?" On the one hand, an apple is just an apple, a single piece of fruit from a little tree, but an apple is an ever-changing experience dependent on the partaker. In that same way poetry is just poetry—as the dictionary says, "literary work in metrical form"—but, poetry is defined differently depending on the poet. I felt the need to rephrase the question to move toward **my** definition of great poetry.

Finding one's own meaning for great poetry is oftentimes a difficult endeavor, much like locating a label for life. After almost two hours of pondering, I tossed the quest aside and began to leaf through a collection of poetry I had just received for my birthday. I passed selections of Dickenson and Neruda, poems of love and sonnets of rain; I was searching for something, an answer or maybe just a line to pull me from the question. It was then that I came across a poem on which I had underlined almost half and drawn several little hearts. The poem was "Late Hours" by Lisel Mueller. I read over the poem for a second time. A bit frustrated, I blankly skimmed down to the end, and thought to myself, "So what? It's just a collection of captured moments!" I threw my hand down on the page, somehow trying to dismiss the poem from my presence.

I looked out at the snowy day, sighed and brought my gaze back down to the partly veiled page. The title and the last words of the lines were the only things sticking out from under my hand. I read the sequence of exposed poetry: "Late Hours… world, earshot, swish, siren, us, nights, bedroom, fragmented, go, birth, windows, Chekov, world, happy, grieve, lives." I was instantly struck with a feeling of the sweet "late hours" of the night and I couldn't help but smile. I remembered how much my teachers used to go on and on about being selective with line breaks, but this was the first time I realized just how important it actually was. This poem, just in the words it was divided on, caught me off guard and took me to a beautiful, familiar place.

I realized the power and honesty of this poet to have gone within herself and found the very essence of what it felt like to be awake in the "late hours" of a summer night in a big city. The words on which the lines broke were the purest and simplest state of this poem, and every poem. Reading the line breaks of the poem was like reading the outline of a book. Once I felt a grip on the essence of the poem, I realized why I had cast it aside so quickly: it is a poem meant for the slow "late hours." It was not one to be scanned over quickly in a harsh manner (not that any poem is), but I realized that I was not going to understand it fully unless I looked at it through the eyes of the speaker. The speaker in this case, "the eye of the poem" as Francis Mayes calls it, is a peaceful individual drifting in and out of sleep in the calm environment of home, while the crazy outside world drifts in and away.

With this in mind, I went back and read it over again slowly and softly. I became extremely touched. I recalled my original thought about this poem being, "a simple collection of captured

Leah Marie Waller

moments" and I realized I was right, but that did not diminish its significance—it made it that much more profound. For what are the memories of life that we hold precious? Our first date, our first kiss, the first time we broke the speed limit and got caught—it is all just a "collection of captured moments." I read over the section that I had underlined:

voices float into our bedroom,

lunar and fragmented,

as if the sky had let them go

long before our birth.

The palpable perfume of that moment in which one hears voices from the street or upstairs apartment is perfectly captured. It makes me remember my long sleepless nights, with their pleasures and pains. I can feel them and am taken back to moments that were over ten years ago. A great poet's work make you feel at home by capturing a moment and immortalizing it, allowing custom access to a perfectly preserved experience, even to those who have never shared the same moment.

After all that I received from this first poem, I was extremely interested to look at more of Lisel Mueller's work. I flipped to the index of my book and saw that she authored several other poems. I turned to page 224, where I found the poem "Hope." I was instantly intrigued by the title and began reading it in good faith that it was going to be excellent. I was not disappointed. Unlike "Late Hours," however, my admiration for this poem was immediate. I wondered why; looking over the stanzas out of context, nothing struck me as extraordinary. The subject makes the poem gripping. Having an abstract subject such as hope balanced the simple yet concrete style of the poem.

Definitions of hope vary from person to person, but many seem to share the common theme of a sense of distance or impossibility. In this poem, however, Mueller seems to have captured an intangible idea in concrete form. I can still feel the depth of the subject, but do not have to experience it as an untouchable spirit of the clouds. Rather, upon reading this poem, hope has become a potential firsthand experience.

Each line of the poem seemed to hit my soul like a little spark of hope. I felt inspired, and quickly pulled out a sheet of paper and a pen. As I pressed my inky wand into the page to craft the first line, I suddenly became scared. How could I capture hope? And even if I did, would anyone really be able to pull the same meaning from my words? I felt a tight pinch in my heart. Perhaps I did not possess the necessary skill to sculpt the abstract. Maybe if I wrote a poem about hope it would just wind up a dry-mouthed lisp unable to voice her purpose. Then I read the last lines of the poem: "it is this poem, trying to speak."

It was as if a good friend and I had just said our favorite ice cream at the same time. Mueller's poem was able to accomplish the rare feat of extending out from the page like soft arms to me, the open-hearted reader. I sat there and even though I knew nothing about her history, I felt like I knew who she was.

When a friend told me that the poet Emily Dickinson had a boring life, I instantly responded harshly. Although he only meant Dickinson's personal history, I was still peeved. Sure she may have been simple and a bit anti-social but her mind must have been a country with roads leading in all directions! What many people do not realize is that when you read a poem, past the stanzas and lines, beneath meaning and metaphor, is the soul of the poet. When I enjoy something in a poet's work, I am savoring years of his or her history and hours of wistful futures. I felt this way when I was struck by Mueller's poetry and I think it is what everyone experiences when reading a *great* poem.

Inside My Pen

Inside my pen is a small lake
in Keosauqua
where oily gray fish
are nodding their tails.

In the ink that flows through my pen
is the taste of a wine from 1947
and the smell of Thai food on Fridays.

I've got a sloppy kiss in a movie theatre
and an insult that lead to a heart break
in my pen.

You would never have guessed
that pressed inside the tiny walls of my pen
was the smell of the New Jersey Boardwalk in August
or the taste of sushi in Texas

In my pen is the ashen breath of bon fires across closed eyes
and burning legs of a three mile cross country hero.

Who knew life could fit
inside this little black wand
that casts no more than a hair
of a shadow on the page?

The Song of March

The late March rain is a shy, beautiful woman
who spends her hours stirring silver spoons
through fat mugs of dark hot chocolate
and snuggles feather quilts about the limbs of chilly bodies.

I awake to her ghostly hands pressing the panes of my bedside
  window
looking in with the soft hush of transparent eyes.

The late March rain is an endless secret rain
with a tiny voice from a million mouths
that slides into the mind like an Irish flute.

Leah Marie Waller

Tuck In The Clouds

Across the belly of skinny Iowa
the morning has just begun the stretch

The fields are yawning and the stars
are off to work
The pilot has turned off
the seat belt sign
and I am free
to move about the cabin.

Hurry while the sky
is still vacant.

Sailing Without A Clock

Oh let us lose the lake
and linger lambent in the wind.
To slip the sash of the sunset on our smiles
and curl the crooked Earth with crawfish fins.
Don't find your forever in the crumbling isles,
the waves of the walnut, or the wake of the sea,
but ride it down breezes, past the rake of the black.
Leave your ticking troubles—sore with me,
let loose the want for all the world we lack.

Leah Marie Waller

Birth of a Poem

Poetry met me
under a willow tree
on the cuffs of an Iowa river.
I was scared
but he kissed my wrists
and told me that everything
would be alright.
He removed my clothes
slowly,
a sock,
then a sleeve.
So smooth I didn't know
I was naked
until the March breeze
laughed across my back.

I reached for something
to cover myself
but everything I grabbed
was just more and more
of him.
I had no choice
but to embrace him,
lest I expose my nakedness
any longer.

He was warm,
light, tender, and romantic.
So many kinds of delicious
I thought I should explode.
I spun, ran, ducked and dipped
in and out of reality.
Kissing the bends and joints
of my sudden desire.
Then I opened my eyes
and he was gone.

My mother told me I was foolish
to lie with a lover
who held thousands of hearts.
"Did you think he would stop for you?"
she asked.

My soul began to grow round and plump
over the next nine mouths.
I had decided
to put it up for adoption
when it was born.
I had no job
and no house
after all,
I could never support
such a thing.

It was a rainy morning
when the writing contractions began.
Closer and closer together,
shorter and shorter lines.
I felt pain
but I would not take drugs.
Pleasure,
though I screamed.
Suddenly the tiny thing burst out
caught by the gloved white hands
of the page.

My small bloody poem,
coughing and gasping desperately
for life.
I stared down at it.
Into the large blue eyes
of poetry
and I knew
in every batten
of my being
that this scroll
this flesh
of my flesh
was the answer
to life.

I Want To Write A Great Poem

I wanted to write a great poem!
The kind that makes you wiggle your toes
before bed
or wake up
before the alarm.
But I'm afraid,
afraid that this well of passion
won't make it onto the page.
Every time I try and make this poem about something
it doesn't feel good enough for itself.

I tried to write about that cold still lake
I swam in last Saturday,
the slow sighs of the evening
and the glow of the yellow fields behind the barn,
but it just didn't seem good enough
for this poem.

I tried to write about those moments
in the car yesterday
after lunch
just after I turned off the engine,
watching the last drops of the icicles
fall from the edge of handy cap sign.
For all the silence that moment held
it is still not enough for this poem.

Leah Marie Waller

No, this poem must be a special poem,
filled with the mystery
of a still cove,
and the longing
of an empty desert
but somehow—
I lack the courage
to write it.

The Wake Of The Lilacs

Lilacs
I walk
You strike me
I fall
You catch me
Drowning in the dreamy aroma
Purple passion pulls me
Resistance
Exacerbation
Porous I let go
You seep into me
Through my blood
Filling my heart
Soothing my soul
Languid lack of logic
Lost in lilac land, living love
Engulf my senses
Now I see
What fuels your perfumes
Is me

Leah Marie Waller

As I Walked Upon Meditation

Walking upon meditation
the world falls to whispers.
The dry December pavement
curves round the country houses
like moats of rainy dreams.
Past the sunlit rooftops
as I trip unexpectedly
into the coupled numbers of adolescence,
the hand of the great seer
softly beckoned.
I can't say from where
his medium peach fingers extended,
but I suddenly found myself in the skin
of a person I didn't recognize
but desperately wanted to meet.

The Poets Voice

One cricket playing
in an empty house—
the sound of silence

Leah Marie Waller

The Summer

When an impulse of awareness falls into that unbounded ocean of being naturally and immediately the heart flows into poetry.

—Maharishi Mahesh Yogi

Every year towards the end of July, when it gets too hot to breathe, my family and I shove our lives into suitcases and fly up the coast to the cool rocky shores of Maine. I can always smell the difference in the air as soon as I step off the plane: a thick, seedless watermelon scent that fills my soul with mystery. The look in the eyes of every local resident is 100 years older then their body and the shadows of the full dark pine trees cut the view like wild icicles.

In the heart of Great Island, my grandparents' incredible house stretches across the damp ground like an enormous smile. No matter how wide or tall the buildings I walk into may be, they never feel as vast as the original Johnson home.

The unforgettable time spent in Maine cannot be measured in weeks, days or hours. No, I have been there enough to know that time stands still on the Island, so still that all guests, however preoccupied, are forced to take at least one moment for their inner selves.

On the Shores of Maine

On the fingernail of Great Island
we walked barefoot
over the kindly sleeping sand.
The sun elbowed its way through the rain clouds
and watched with curious rays.
Waves gave up their crashing;
seagulls surrendered the food
and the whole world looked through my eyes to you.

We picked where our house,
where our hammock would be—
"Someday when we have the money, of course."
The pine breath of the trees
weighed down the morning air.
We claimed a large rock
in your name, watched white sails
invade the blue horizon.
I curled my toes around your pant leg,
and the hands of your love touched my hair.

Call Me From A Coconut

White beach, palm leaf—
the water would look like Gaderade,
the sky would taste like salad.
Call me from a coconut
and we'll run the waves together.

Coffee roast, island toast—
we'd always go barefoot
and wake with the tide.
Call me from a coconut
and we'll run the waves together

Flower crowns, grass skirt towns
our bed would sound like summer
our smiles would grow like mangos
Call me from a coconut
and we'll run the waves together

Sea shell phones and driftwood scones
gulls would snipe our sandwiches
as we sipped out the hours with pineapple straws
Call me from a coconut
and we'll run the waves together

Leah Marie Waller

Fish n' chips and salty lips
time turns our toes to prunes
and fattens our wallets with sand dollars
Call me from a coconut
and we'll run the waves together

Sailing to Ragged Island

We all sail out in tiny boats of oak.
The tide is high and wind kicks at our backs
while every seal removes its seaweed cloak
and watches us with ocean eyes of wax.
The water parts and fleeting buoys drown,
but we move towards the rock where clams reside
(and treasure grandpa claims he almost found.)
In Zip-lock, tuna sandwiches confide
to salted chips and vats of mint ice tea.
My aunties laugh, enticed by misty trails,
while uncles pride in raking through the sea,
Our Raged Isle approaches through the vale.
We guide our sails abreast the rippled cove
and slide our souls inside the Island's glove

Leah Marie Waller

Moon Lashes

Bent over the stone balcony
down by the lake
her pale arms
surprised the darkness
with their tall graceful strides.

Her dress hung organically
about her hips
like strands of green
cotton leaf
and the hungry south wind
rippled her hair
like dark spaghetti.

I watched as she pulled
the mysterious night in
with long slow breaths
and when she turned
the moon fell
onto her forehead,
rolled of her lashes,
and bounced
like a sleepy silver dream
into my palms.

Summer Pantoum

As I tan, topless, soaked in sunscreen on a rooftop in July
Mowers fan juicy grass clippings onto cracked streets
Boys clack bats to softballs and mothers sip lemonade
Middle-aged men wash motorcycles and tend barbecues

Mowers fan juicy grass clippings onto cracked streets
Moist lips melt remainders of vanilla ice cream cones
Middle-aged men wash motorcycles and tend barbecues
College beatniks tinker rose wood guitars for quarters

Moist lips melt remainders of vanilla ice cream cones
Oak trees quiver cricket quarrels and cicada symphonies
College beatniks tinker rose wood guitars for quarters
Chins trickle with tears from triangular watermelon wedges

Oak trees quiver cricket quarrels and cicada symphonies
A club of pierced rebels graffiti the west walls of a factory
Chins trickle with tears from triangular watermelon wedges
Seven-year-olds jump rope down freshly paved drives

A group of pierced rebels graffiti the west walls of a factory
A green-thumbed grandmother weeds a walkway of lilies
Seven-year-olds jump rope down freshly paved drives
Summer rays hit a girl's hair and a boy falls in love

Leah Marie Waller

A green-thumbed grandmother weeds a walkway of lilies
Hands of chubby babies chase herds of oval bubbles
Summer rays hit a girl's hair and a boy falls in love
Time moves as slowly as cold molasses across toast

Ocean Dance

See this wild dancer
turn in the hands
of New England
grandmothers.

Watch her shore line
as she dips
with her chilling
turquoise lips
onto the white beaches
of Maine.

The misty
morning fog
rolls in
when she tosses
of her layered
grey gipsy skirt,
and as her salty limbs crash
into the ends
of the islands
she bleeds
perfect sunsets.

Leah Marie Waller

Green Eyed Sestina

You watched me as I turned 20, with your soft green
eyes. Held by the gentle breast of a milky candle
the only words that could be made out were in the shaky
   harmony
of the lyrics by Bob Dylan. Down my cheeks the tears
ran into each other. Back stage from your apartment moaned
   the train,
and I felt the square sections of your new, high thread count
   comforter against my skin.

You plucked your new guitar strings, which vibrated against
   my skin
like tiny crickets humming under a green
moon. The thin window glass shook as the evening train
puffed on it's harmonica. The dying teenage candle
was the only crutch to help our eyes. Outside like bridal tears
the snow danced to the earth from the white pink and yellow
   clouds in harmony.

On the bed our pale feet were woven in perfect harmony
the only reminder of my body, the soft touch of your skin.
Your looks tapped on my hearts small drum in a leak of tears
and with your iris paint brush turning, you stroked my world
   green.
My hair curled by the tiny fingers of the candle
and in dissonance with the song we sang squeaked the excited
   train.

Fading as it left the town came the call of the winter train.
You never seemed to mind that I kept salting the harmony.
You played like morning would never come and the flame
    danced in the candle.
My soul went beyond the redistricting walls of my skin.
From the window shone the street lamp once golden now was
    green,
it fell on your jaw and shoulder like tiny clover tears

You sang more but my notes could only be a silent rain of tears.
Your voice rose up and echoed like the calling of the train,
your passion blazing like Ireland green.
The low male tone of your heart with the high female of mine
    made harmony.
My eyes grew heavy with the weight of music on their skin,
and soon I lost all sight of the room clothed by the candle.

Still within my darkness I felt the flicker of the candle.
you stopped playing but music stayed, in the sound of
    dripping wax tears.
You blew out the drumming flame, still I felt the beat in my
    skin.
My senses boarded the last departing train
and soon all creation was in harmony,
nothing but a deep and fading green—

A lone green candle,
burning in harmony like the dying tears
of the last nightly train falling on the skin of God.

Ode to My Foot

                              And then
                    The 3 he 4   At last to the
            The 2 Who I Who One who is to
     To   That is Know Tries to the toe
     The Always Takes Be so To rule
     Tiny There wear tall Them all
This is the sole who takes the heat all day long
The one who smells the socky, stink-pressing song
Who goes to the beat of his own heart-felt tune
Whose curves may shine in the light of the moon
Fits to in eight and a half when taken in shoe size
A wild outdoor hunter with balls and nails for eyes
And as this flesh will move from place to place
It never fails to do it with full forced grace
And if I choose to climb over a garden wall
I know this friend would never let me fall
It's of much help when driving in the car
Good for the distance short and fair
It's the first to feel a watery touch
When I go back to the sea shore
Holds my weight, doesn't ask much
No body could ask for anything more
It's ran me through the finish lines
Elegant when in dress shoes it dines
Light in travels, a pilot at heart
A steady worker from the start
Ready to kick anyone in the way
His effort always helps the day
Strong to the touch, to the eye
Who when I fall goes to the sky
Able to heal from any bad blow
Winter will chill it with the snow
In the hot summer it may go bare
Large high heels will give it a wear
Always growing as the years pass
Larger by toe and larger by mass
Makes a very good bug squasher
(Be sure to put socks into washer)
Everything you ever need it—
To be, I know it's always
There for me, I thank—
You, my wonderful
F O O T

Leah Marie Waller

Finding Maine

Maine is in the pine trees
I smell blueberry waffles ironed by love
My Aunts are laughing like sisters
I taste my turkey sandwich
Who drank all the chocolate milk?
Maine is in the pine trees
Watermelon breezes kiss my pace
Grandpa's morning, evening afternoon, 2am, and for no
   reason coffee fills the air
My cousins are making pool war with cannon balls
Butter hints to ocean lobster
Maine is in the pine trees
Seagulls laugh with a sarcastic squawk
Needle paths cringle to my every foot
Newborn babies fill the air
Cold water chills me to God
Maine is in the pine trees

Lake Rathbun With Dad

The red sun sank into the horizon
leaving streams of fruit punch
across the lake.
Dad and I sat below the mini cliffs
with tuna and watermelon
listening to the current
meet the artificial sand,
and trying to hear the ocean.
"Once upon a time…"
Dad began as he threw some dry oak
on the thirsty bon fire.
"and Sir Kay was the greatest archer…"
I moved across the fake beach to the water
shaking slightly on the uneven ground.

Dad held Hobyone from drifting
and I climbed onto the black netting
and moved towards the center of the boat.
We rippled out in the dark,
and Dad continued his story.
"Unima flew past the dark river
and up to The Mountains of the Moon."
His soft words reached across my imagination
and into my view of the little dipper.
I tried to hold on
but knew that I was getting too old
for this sort of thing.

Leah Marie Waller

Reminding Mira

I trekked down the needled path
carrying two empty plastic water bottles
and several Ziploc bags;
I was bringing Maine home
to my sister
in Iowa.

Above me old pines leaned
into each other
like batting lashes
and ambitious light
fell into sporadic dance.

Six leaves of wintergreen—
bitter, spry and refreshing:
I placed a few into a bag.
Mira must remember the wintergreen.

I scaled a tiny slope,
up to the highest point of my walk.
To my right the trees opened
unveiling a small patch of ocean
no bigger than my thumb.
I pulled a small limb from a lone branch
that hung over the trail and put it into a bag;
the bark responded with a dense, sticky drool.
Mira must remember the trees.

The walk began its steep decline to the water.
I grasped bellies of stable trunks
and clenched my treasures.

I veered right,
towards the spring,
a crucial ingredient.
The ancient well sat waiting for me
in a small melon-sized pool.
I greeted it with one of my bottles,
grazing only the surface
to respect the dusty spirits below.
Mira must remember the sweet, cold taste.

The woods were so dense
I wondered if they might swallow me
but at last they surrendered the little cove.

I climbed down a small wooden ladder
and stepped cautiously onto the rocks.
Before me great Atlantic thrashed
her wild mane of foamy hair
and I had to make sure Mira remembered.
I knelt down and presented my bottle
as a vessel for a single strand of salty esteem.

Leah Marie Waller

Only the view remained then,
but how to capture a view?
I picked up the largest of my bags
and opened it wide.
I spread my arms
and danced my empty sack
across the expanse.
I twirled it to the ocean
and bowed it to the sky.
Then I pulled it to my breast
and sealed it tightly.
Maine was coming home with me,
Mira will remember.

Early One Saturday

It was early
one Saturday
late July
on Baily Island.
We awoke and left
before any one else
in the house was awake,
which, as you know, is unusual
for us.

We picked up lunch
at that cute place on the corner,
Sam's, I think it was called.
I got the tuna on wheat
and you got the smoked turkey on rye,
both to go.

We drove our little car onto the mainland
just as the sun was coming up
over the foggy morning pines.

I still can't believe
we got that great parking spot
right in the second row.
You wheeled the cooler behind you
and I carried the chairs.

Leah Marie Waller

We walked slowly down the path
there was no reason to hurry,
not today.

It was a full rich tide and the view
was still heavy with mist
but we knew that only made it better.

Then for a hundred
and eighty three minutes
we just sat there,
watching the waves turn
and the sky clear.
Only brief words,
small kisses
and light hugs.
The salt water fell over itself,
and the metal feet of our chairs
burrowed into the sand.
And somewhere in there
we heard our lives
down generations of beaches
and through decades of oceans.

Poetic Confidence

Climb Mount Fuji O snail, but slowly, slowly.

—Kobayashi Issa

If you are searching for writing reassurance, the best thing that I can tell you is to keep writing. Even if you feel incompetent and are sure that whatever you scratch onto the sad little page is bound to be worthless, do not give up. Your mind like a muscle, powerful and packed with potential, but without regular use, becomes sloppy and weak. Even if you only write a little every day, you will find yourself gaining strength with time. In the same way you start persisting in writing to improve, you must continue writing regularly if you expect to remain a good writer. There is never a time when you should stop exercising your talent, no matter how stupendous you think you are.

I will never forget how fantastically cocky I became my freshmen year in high school. After years of writing couplets about the young men and women in my grade, I had been dubbed the class poet. I strolled about the halls feeling ridiculously pleased with myself until the day I was taken down a notch.

It was second period English. The teacher was handing back our poetry homework, and I was so lost in my own vanity that I hardly noticed that mine was resting on my desk. Suddenly the rosy hues and silver sparkles faded and a big fat C came into focus. I was furious. As soon as class was over, I pulled the teacher aside to protest—surely it was a mistake. After I had finished my teenage rant, I looked over and noticed that my teacher was smiling. "Leah", she said, "your poem was very sweet, but sweet is all I have seen from you and I know that you are capable of more. So before you take offense, go home and see what more you can put into this poem. Cut it down and take the reader to the heart of what you are really trying to say."

I did take offense, but I was determined to show her that I was impeccable, so I took the poem home and worked on it. That night I took my first steps towards becoming a true poet. I stretched my creativity, swept my standards and by the end of it all I had a work of literature that I was proud of.

Since that poem, I have never stopped pushing my writing limits. Whenever I don't feel confident or begin to doubt myself, I reach for the next branch and seek to become better. I have found that doubt is only a limb of fear, and as long as I keep an upper hand on the next step, I have no reason to be afraid of falling.

Invisible Hours

I can hear the slow seconds
humming by and taste their lazy fruit.
Somewhere in those invisible hours
between sleeping and dreaming
you pulled me towards you,
and like a shy petal
I curled to your touch.

A small car passed,
a heavy train moaned,
and I fell in love with you
all over again
without ever opening my eyes.

In The Twill Hammock

I lie in my twill hammock
by the lake at dusk.
Pink salmon fries in fat
over a small camping stove.
The late-shift wind wanders
through the Cotton Woods.
A tired, middle-aged couple arrives
in a brown van with a tan door
to take the spot down by the showers.
The fading whiz of motorboats
stretches across the lake
like a beer-bottled topless good time.
It grows cooler,
as the dreary sun rolls to her bed
in lacey pink lingerie
and a purple wig.
The scents of avocados, red peppers, and feta
waltz over from the wooden salad bowl.
On the rectangular timber
tropical flames hiss
as they pull out the perspiration
like a cigar puffing ash.

I know that eventually
I'll eat,
take a naked swim
in the infant ocean,
and pitch myself in a red
and gray-poled pyramid
under the freckled sky.
I know eventually I'll dream
and eventually I'll wake
to pack the melting cooler,
to roll my dirty blue sleeping bag
and ponytail my smoky hair.
Eventually getting into a car
on the way to responsibility,
no longer just a limb
of the woods and the water.
Eventually Lord,
but right now
I just want to lie
on the edge of predictability
in my twill hammock
with your silk and cloudy arms
sustaining me
in possibility.

Smores

The earth has opened iron lips to sigh
out a series of orange belly dancers
with red feather hats.
Logs hiss and pop
their wooden knuckles.
A trio of marshmallows
rest in the middle of the scene
like tired sumo wrestlers tanning.
An anatomy of chocolate lies stiffly
on a graham cracker bed.
The fire shushes itself
as a blue halo hovers tentatively.
The marshmallows are suddenly lifted.
They cushion on a coco plane
and the three elements meld into one module.
The smore hums its existence
for a moment
and then a mouth devours
like a sunrise ingesting the stars.

Laundry Day Ranga

Oak tree tosses
a leafy skirt—
the ballet begins

Three leafed trumpets—
ode to the clover

I scribe the OM on the leaf—
holy leaf, holy leaf, holy leaf—
you   me   God's feet

The ant climbs grass leaves
looking for the one that leads to heaven.

The sky is naked,
perhaps the clouds
are in the wash.

The grass blade—
a thread in God's coat.

The cottonwood trees
sway alcoholically
into each other.

Yellow butterfly turns off
in the shade.

Leah Marie Waller

A Word For My Mother

You were the hug when everyone was crying.
You called when the boys didn't.
You paid for all the things
I never told you
I always wanted.
You pulled my shoulders back
and my spirit up
when I didn't believe in myself.
You taught me how to bake cookies
and how to make a family.
You nourished me
so I could nourish him.
You will always be
the most beautiful woman in the world.
Since the beginning
the mountains of your heart
echoed down on me
an unwavering note.
So I just have one thing to say:
I love you mom,
you gave me life.

The Fall

Write as though you had in your hand the last pencil on earth.

—Unknown

Every autumn I declare that fall is my favorite season and every spring I change my mind, but in all honesty there is something amazing about the fall. Fall is like the tea before the nap, the belly before the birth or the pen before the word. It is a season pregnant with potential. When I step outside in the fall it is as if poems and stories are tumbling out of the sky and plump on the boughs of every tree.

There was this large sugar maple on the south edge of my hometown and every October it would turn a fantastic red color. The leaves would dance in the wind like a shredded gypsy skirt and fall to the ground in stages like some epic grand finale. I never seem to be in need for things to write as the summer reaches for winter.

Flattering Light

I couldn't watch it but I saw it, in the green or the brown of
  your eyes
Couldn't say it but I meant it betwixt the creamy lies

It had never been so quiet with bold bass lines all around
His lost lips touched mine and the stillness turned to sound

New chords through ears held closed for so long
New love to the tune of a "Green Day" song

Perfect pitch by your side in our Nisan four-doored
with the windows rolled down for the wind-rushing roar

What I saw in the iris of your turning mind that day
Was a poem that kissed back with a life time display.

A Dream

My hair is curly from a tightly pinned bun
the damp brunette waves tangle across the cotton pillows
and cold sighs fall off the thin windows.
My day trips drunkenly into a slow orange dream.
Arizona mixed in a desert bowl
stained with the sunset and spiced with cactus sugar.
In my dream I ride a horse that the dusk paints black
and kick the wind that falls off the boney hills
with my dancing hair.
The phone rings suddenly
and the dream
is lost.

Leah Marie Waller

Even the Grass Has a Shadow

Today I went running after work,
a soft rhythmic kind of a jog.
My feet pounded the cracked pavement
like heavy rubber drums
and every breath chilled my flaming mind
like sighs of fresh cucumber.
In that moment
scaling the back roads of Iowa
the sun leaned so kindly on the Earth
that even the grass
had a shadow.

My Body

Body
I strive to balance you
between obedient and wild.
I trip you, skin you and bleed you,
make you an outcast and tease you to tears.
I run you through finish lines
against the wind to steal fourth place.
I've plumped and dieted you
curled you, healed you, made you up
and with a corsage and a velvet dress I took you to prom.

Now I walk you around parks
in long mysterious strides
and demand the secrets of life
on a small playground swing.
I dirty you with days of sleeping in
and bleach you with lavender bubble baths.
I sail you across Lake Rathbun,
pole you up and stake you down for a shelter wherever I
choose.
I spend thirty dollars on your sushi, but won't spare quarters
to do your laundry.
I swim you in the wavy salty potato chip ocean
and fry you like a toasted cheese on the beach.

And when you get older, body,
I will plow you and rake you and put seeds in you.
I'll mock you brown haired and blue eyed
into a James or a Rebecca.
I'll pluck you into music and dip you into dance.
I'll nurse you, educate you and love you even when you break
the rules.

And my body when you are complete
with money and fame and a next generation
I'll retire you in a house rectangular and purple.
Then as you rest there finished, three-storied and sea stormed,
I'll crash on the beach next to you
dance in the air around you
and never care to live in you.

In The Large Booth

We three sit in the "large" booth
in the smoking section,
though none of us smokes.
One of you in a "whatever" outfit,
with beautiful unwashed hair
pulled back by a broken rubber band.
The other in a Hawaiian shirt,
the first three buttons open to a wife-beater,
short light brown hair,
falling to a slight Elvis curl in the front,
over clear-rimmed glasses.
Me with dark jeans, and a low cut light blue top,
my hair pulled tightly back in a clipped bun.
One of you plays with your unwashed hair,
sipping down the bottomless coffee.
The other tells me a story,
"Once at Subway…"
My eggs are undercooked; though the entertainment
seems to override the disappointment.
"Pass the ketchup."
There is a disagreement about the Subway story.
The waitress with the ten-day makeup is back.
"No, just water for me, thank you."
The carefree Subway story has become a heated discussion.
I am confused, so I just keep smiling,
sipping cold water.

Leah Marie Waller

"NO! You don't understand! You're making no sense!"
I take the last bite of runny egg and sit back.
The discussion ends and both parties apologize.
I keep sipping and smiling.
Next time I will ask for less ice.
The waitress stares, beats her foot,
and rubs her pencil
on the green order pad.
We all check our watches,
knowing we have to be somewhere.
I want the coffee, Subway, and runny eggs to last,
but one of you has to meet that "Stupid boy!"
Whom you're head over heals for.
I have miscalculated my brunch cost,
I ask for a spare dollar,
one of you groans,
"OK, but this is my laundry money."

Decaf in the Dark

Nothing to this Friday night
but this tall cup of French Roast.
Sip one, my hair is curly
sip two, my legs are shaven
sip three, nothing on thirty-two channels.
Sip ten, I can hear first loves laughing
across the city
and first kisses calling the moon.
Sip ten, the 28th man I kissed
stole my lips.
Something about the way his shoulders
hummed his sultry intentions
behind his cardboard cup.
Sip thirteen, the ocean
made me feel like flying
this year,
it was so high
on the mist of its own flesh
that it must have found the moon.
Sip sixteen, it's hot for May.
Sip nineteen, I'm drunk on the late hour.

Leah Marie Waller

Tickled

Seed puff prickles
with the soft energy
of life

A Time To Rhyme

Life is too important to be taken seriously.

—Oscar Wilde

There are many people who, despite the surge of modern open form poetry, still prefer that classic rhyming poem. In my early days of poetry the adorable cupboard of the rhyming couplet was as far as my talents stretched. It got so bad that at one point my English teacher demanded that she did not want to see another poem that rhymed until I had produced a decent one that did not. Never the less, there is an unmistakable charm in a poem that can properly pull off a decent rhyming scheme.

The first thing to remember when writing rhyming poetry is that the most obvious sounds are not always the best ones (unless you're Dr. Suess.) If you can't seem to think of unique words to end your line with, the easiest way to avoid sounding cliché is to fill the middle of the line with an excellent metaphor/simile or image. In this way, you can use easy-to-rhyme simplistic words at the end but keep your verse zesty! For example, rather than stating:

A jar that's large and tall
that's filled with lots of ink
and every single wall
is painted in hot pink.

It is much better to write something like:

A tattered cup with eighty pens,
each pulping endless ink
and stain glass windows streaming purple
tossed in shades of pink.

This allows the reader to get so caught up the images that they forget the line contains the simple little rhyme of "ink" to "pink."

You can also use rhyming as a tool to lighten up a poem. In Walt Whitman's poem "O Captain My Captain" he uses rhyming to turn the tragic memoir of George Washington's death into heartfelt masterpiece.

The rhythm and melody of great rhyming poem turns any reader into a musician. When I read Longfellow's *Psalm of Life* or Masefield's *Sea Fever* I feel more like I am voicing notes than speaking words. I told my friend that I wished I was a great musician, and she said, "but you are, you're a great poet." So the next time someone asks you to sing puff up your lungs and recite your favorite Shakespeare sonnet.

Freckle Riddle

Naked 'neath the hips,
haphazard pebble pricks.
Brown and yellow
they fleck this Cello,
humming nothing—
always giggling.

Sunrays flock
to chicken
this pock—
but not an infection
for science to question.

Semi-Sweet
skin chipped treat
but never eat
though dough is meat.

These beach bum friends
relax on me,
strokeless paint
their galaxy.

Leah Marie Waller

Tickle trickle
on breast, bum
and knuckles.
Cover me!
Cover me!
My small citrus
truffles!

Feeding Cats

I pull into the driveway
listening tentatively for soft paws
on the dew covered grass.
I call their names
they do not answer.
The movement sensor light
comes on
and I gasp
slightly.
I slide my copy of the key
into the fake gold knob
and twist.

I grab a can of Newman's Own cat food
and a feeding plate

Soon I can just make out
the first pair of yellow eyes
ascending on the horizon.

Leah Marie Waller

They plant themselves around the small green dish
poking their bumpy tongues
at the wet lump
and it slowly vanishes.
They press their bellies
into my knees
and rub their faces
on my hands.

I look towards the dark woods
and the hush of some ancient tong
whispers to me
Suddenly I just want to run
through those black thickets all night,
to catch the small animals there
in my mouth,
and be a part of the mystery
that goes on while I am usually
sleeping.

Thursday Fog

The clouds have fallen onto the world
like silver velvet veils
and every turned and tainted mind
is lost in fairytales.

The woods are not the trees today
nor is the road a street,
for every damp and dirty shoe
has sky beneath its feet.

Leah Marie Waller

Purple

Mysterious dark and knotted
the chilly tangled damsel
lost in the strange summer frost
finds her way home
from the gnarled forest.
Here she hushes herself
into an unwavering dream.
Where wizards are shaking hands with universes
and she never has to wake.
Never waking so as long as the boats
under her feet
and the waves
of her long cloak
whisper
in purples.

Listen To Your Grandfather

Speak slowly little child
the wind is too fast
the road, the mind
and the whispers are too fast.

Come here little child
sit on my knee
hug my old heart
the summer and the sun
and the tide are too fast.

I see you little child
in your quite little world
no need to rush
no need to worry
Kiss the crown
of my balding head
and walk your life
down a beach of smiles.

Leah Marie Waller

Driving

Acres of lion mane grain
melting into silver snake creeks.
Veggie berry blanket bundled roadside stands.
Open northern aurora gusts reaching pungent peeks.
24, 45, 60 miles this hour...

Dirty drunken trucks downshifting drones,
amateur asses hanging out pickup windows.
Mini lakes and potty breaks
and sacrificed frozen gutter does.
35, 52, 66 miles this hour...

Hawaiian t-shirt tourists
photographing phony Sasquach tracks
kinky curb ridden cops call it a warning if you're cute
pulp free, margarine feeding pancake shakes
45, 63, 70 miles this hour...

Calling moms, messages and men
closing in, moments eroded
back seat trio tucks in after ten
our hearts are home, our memories unloaded
six, seven hundred, eight-hundred thousand hours this life time.

Winter

The spider gains the liberty of space by means of its own thread.

—Upanishads

I admit that winter has never been my favorite season. When freezing rain is careening against my face at 40 mph and I cannot feel my toes, I am unhappy, to say the least. However, the winter season carries an irreplaceable touch of magic.

I love the morning after an enormous snow storm, when you can't tell the difference between the road and the grass. I step out onto my powdered porch and everything is so still I feel as though I am the only human being in the world. The flakes condense under my wide shoes with a muffled crunch and if only for a moment the world feels united.

Graveyard

Histories exhale from beneath the grass
told by a collection of personalized rocks—
mothers, fathers, and children.
I, half dead,
to feel alive
console the abstruse dead.
Planting myself, beneath the evergreen eyelashes,
I try to acre the wisdom of "Tarrence."
His mark is a magical font pressed to a backyard stone.
Quiet and honest,
someone who did everything once and right.
Hand me my afflatus Tarrence!
With your earth eaten hands,
ink the sole of my pen!

Looking At My Grandmother

My grandmother's eyes
are island coves
pulling down mountains.

My grandmother's eyes are filled
with green tea and love.

My grandmother's eyes reach
like old pine trees
and smile like snow.

Leah Marie Waller

Soap

The day is finally
over.
I pull the small
blue towel
from the metal rack,
which sings and dances softly
as I move to the sink.
Pulling both ivory
knobs towards me
I stand
fingers in the stream,
waiting for warmth.
I stare
at my hurting features,
which droop and limp
against the hour.
I hit them coldly with the shivering water.
Turning the pink bar beneath the splashes,
the suds emerge.
Putting them against
the oiled and dirtied curves,
I wedge, scrape
pull away
the crumbled clay body
of tears,
stubbed toes

and tucked-in sorrow.
I take handfuls of my neutral friend
And toss him
at the scrubbed, sud-ridden canvas.
My day falls
off
chasing the rose bubbles
down
the
drain.
I lift my head
to see my bare white papered origin,
hundreds of freckles
smiling like orange moons.

Leah Marie Waller

Summer Snow

If it snowed in the summer,
it would snow white winged moths.
I could build an igloo
and sit inside all day,
without the tip of my nose,
or the ends of my fingers
getting cold.
I could make a snowman,
who wouldn't malt
in the morning.
When I went sledding,
it would be like flying
and it wouldn't hurt
when I fell
because the powdered white wings
would be gentle.

Through The Lips

He Pulled my heart out
Through my lips, churned
My blood from toe to wrist, drank
The passion left in me as I lay in bliss
Of ecstasy. Timeless moment
clocked too soon, brush of beard
beneath the moon

Leah Marie Waller

Hero

Little black ant from the oak tree
a suicide jump—
saved by my shoulder

Evening Snow Villanelle

White moths will moan a drunken fall.
Turn the round belly lamp, I'll spin the loom—
and there's always a tarnished silver moon.

If you never answer, they'll never call.
Drink down the day like a Jell-O balloon
White moths will moan a drunken fall.

The night is cloaked beneath this shawl;
Spring awaits in a sheepskin cocoon,
and there's always a tarnished silver moon.

Candle shadows explore each wall
The waving flint n' tinder fire drones.
White moths will moan a drunken fall.

Goose feather covers on bodies left raw.
Let's caress star slinked wrists and make the night swoon--
and there's always a tarnished silver moon.

Oh my sweet love, we're incredibly small.
For the beat of our hearts we've got the right tune.
White moths will moan a drunken fall
and there's always a tarnished silver moon.

Leah Marie Waller

Midnight Fire

Cold-boned travelers kick off the chilly past,
polish your ears and pull the hot chocolate closer
for this story can only be heard by a midnight fire.
The hissing charcoal crackles coughing coal,
the ash of life coats broken brickly bones.
A lonely moan rolls off a flaming tongue
and raspy wording wonders to the room.
Their once was a dancer
who pulled fire from her fan
shook the stars from her skirt
and when the snow turns to sugar
she turns into the dawn
and melts the world.

Inside Secrets

"The difference between the almost-right word and the right word really is a large matter—'tis the difference between the lightning-bug and the lightning."

—Mark Twain

Throughout my years in poetry, I have gained a few particularly useful insights. These are not the Holy Grail of writing, but the sketchy map that led me to my poetic haven.

The first lesson I learned was the most difficult: self-confidence. The first time anyone asked me to perform a poetry reading, I refused. I declared I had nothing worthy of the public ear and walked away. The world was about to let me get away with my stubborn insecurities, when another poet fell suddenly ill and there was no one left to fill the slot, except me. I stood in the left wing of the stage, waiting to go on, with trembling hands and a pounding heart. Then, just as I was sure I would pass out, I looked down at the poem on the first page of my selections. I read it over and smiled. It was a great poem. It was a great poem and I had written it…! The lights fell and the audience let out a soft clap–my cue. I walked across the stage; my black heels clacked on the wooden boards and my grey skirt danced to the rhythm of my stride. I opened with a little joke, how full and sensuous my voice sounded! By the time I began reading I was not sounding words, but voicing confidence. The poems were nice, but my belief in them and my newly discovered self-confidence gave them real, lasting significance.

The second writing epiphany I had was on New Year's Day

of my senior year in high school. Everyday in the preceding week had me staying up consecutively later into the night and by the time the festivities were over on January 1st, it was 5 a.m. Now, I planned an entire day of writing to kick off the New Year, but when the sun woke me up at the bright young hour of 7 a.m., I was well aware of my mistake. Too tired to exercise, I made myself some coffee and broke into my emergency stash of snickers. By 8 a.m., I was jittery from the coffee, crashing from the sugar, and trying to focus my exhausted mind long enough to write a sentence. My greatly anticipated day of creativity was tanked due to my complete disregard for my health. I managed to cram in a pathetic carb-o-licious lunch before crashing into oblivion at 4 p.m. The next morning, I felt horrible. I had lost an entire day. Hours that could have been spent creating new profound poems and fresh short stories had drowned in dreary caffeinated mumbles and confused depression. I was so furious that I turned a complete 180° on my life. I went to bed every night by 9:30 p.m., rarely missed a day of exercise, and began researching protein-balanced meals. Even today, when I begin to lose my inspiration, I seek to find my health and the problem always seems to work itself out.

This last thing may not be for everyone, but I cannot deny the difference it has made in my life. From day one, I have been raised in an oasis of spirituality. Spirituality is a term that has been tossed around for centuries in the mind of mankind. But for me, spirituality is just a means of connecting to the source of one's life, be it God, love, Jesus, or the Unified Field of Quantum Physics. It's pursuing something greater than oneself to find personal truth and meaning. I have found my source through the daily practice of Maharishi Mahesh Yogi's Transcendental Meditation. After studying the major world religion, multiple meditations, yogas, and practices, this is what I have come to love. This is what holds personal enlightenment for me.

These are my three suggestions: confidence, balanced health, and maintaining a connection with your source. When these 3 things are present in my life, my poetry, relationships, creativity, and general existence are their very finest.

A Picture of God

When I pass
into the next world
and arrive
at Your gates—
arthritic, forgetful
and forlorn
with my pale
wrinkled hands outstretched—
what will You look like God?

Will You have a mane
of dove wings
and a chest
of earth?

As You walk
towards me,
will Your legs be the Northern Atlantic,
crashing and foaming
with Your salty divinity?

The arms
that will sway beside You,
will they be two New England
white pines,
needled,
weaving the twilight wind?

Will Your eyes
be a pair of Iowa sunsets
blinking on
and off
the night?

Flying Home From Washington DC

Spinal mountains stretch
across the states,
like scars from some furious sea battle.
The eight lane interstates
and twisting rivers
sprawl out from Pacific to Atlantic.
Strange faces and limbs poke out
of the silence.
A tiny white house
looks up from the crowded hazel forest.
The morning clouds sit on the view
like a cotton night cap.
I think of the first Superman movies
and assume heaven.

Escape to Infinity

Today I am only the ivy
that climes the copper gates of Europe.
Hanging from bud to green to red
and vanishing.

I ride my bobbing thighs
down the milk stained streets
and let the sun lap up my soul.
The sort who speaks only in moans
and finds surrender
on the skirt of a seed puff.

I am bee spit and fruit pulp.
I am jam and August.
If you're cold
wrap me around you a little tighter.
If you're thirsty
put me to your mouth.
I silently remain here
waiting for your sunrise.

Leah Marie Waller

White White White Sox

Too white for the feet of angels
too white for the first snow.
The fresh, crisp, ankle sox
I purchased from Target this morning.
In such snowy bunny fluff
my foot rests like a child
and dances like a Christmas flake.
I move like the daughter of a marshmallow
and who says I can't?

Find Your Inner Poet

Don't be the rider who gallops all night and never sees the horse beneath him.

—Rumi

Every person, whether he or she knows it, has a poet inside. I would be willing to bet that any man or woman has at some point in life created a beautiful poem (that does not mean that it was written down.) Perhaps it was just on a cool day in September as the individual in question was walking through the park and a dark red leaf fell down onto the grey pavement in front of them. The person may have only observed the event for a second, but in that moment a genuine poem was born. Poems are being born all the time but it is those of us who write them down who we call poets—as storytellers, they are simply impelled. Every person's life is filled with poetry. I have created the following exercises to help people capture it:

♠ Go on a walk by yourself and instead of listening to music listen carefully to the world as it passes. Listen to woodpeckers pecking and the paws of a passing dog on the pavement. When you return home describe your walk sound by sound. It doesn't matter if it is long, you can trim it down later.

♠ Sit in a very crowded area such as a mall or large restaurant and create back stories for the people who walk by. Compress each description into a line or two and compile a poem of all the characters.

- Imagine if you had millions of dollars to spend on one room to be designed especially for you. What would the room look, feel, taste and smell like? What would the path to this room be like? How would you enter it?

- Take something that is mostly associated with one sense and describe the sensation for another sense. For example: The sound of strawberries is a baby girl's laughter.

- Write a poem as an ancient friend or relative giving advice to your generation.

- Write a poem as if you were a place such as your hometown, a coffee shop or a certain county.

- Get a dictionary, flip through the pages and with your eyes closed pick out 8 words. Then use those words in a poem.

- Free write (this means without editing or stopping to think) about summer vacation for 30 minutes. Then divide what you wrote into approximate fourths and compress each fourth down to 4 lines.

- Take one of your rhyming poems and remove the rhyming. Then take a poem that doesn't rhyme and add rhyme to it.

So live that your life may be a poem.

—Chang Chao

www.ingramcontent.com/pod-product-compliance
Lightning Source LLC
Chambersburg PA
CBHW031902090426
42741CB00005B/606